BASIC READING SERIES

WORKBOOK
LEVEL C

Six Ducks in a Pond

by Donald Rasmussen and Lynn Goldberg

BASIC READING
BERKELEY·CALIFORNIA

To Parents and Teachers

Donald Rasmussen and Lynn Goldberg developed the BASIC READING SERIES (BRS) in the early 1960s at the Miquon School, a small parent-teacher cooperative near Philadelphia. At that time, most children were taught to read using the "sight" or "look-say" method epitomized by the "Dick and Jane" readers, and many were left behind. Don and Lynn knew there must be a better way, so they spent five years developing their own reading program based on the work of the renowned linguist Leonard Bloomfield. They called their method *inductive whole-word phonics, with a strong linguistics research base.*

After tryouts in inner-city and suburban schools around the country and almost a dozen revisions, the BASIC READING SERIES was published by Science Research Associates (SRA) and enjoyed great success. Over the years, other reading methods have come and then gone out of favor. Now, decades later, phonics is recognized as the scientific approach to reading instruction, and the BASIC READING SERIES is once again available.

BRS is divided into six levels — Levels A to F — with a reader and a workbook for each level. In Level C, children are introduced to 4- and 5-letter words using two consonants in succession, some in which one sound is represented by two letters (digraphs), such as *ll* and *ck*, and others in which two sounds are represented by two letters (blends), such as *sk* and *nd*. At first the two consonants appear at the beginning of words, then at the end of words, and finally at both the beginning and the end. In addition, 36 new exceptional words are introduced.

The BRS Workbooks

The workbooks for BRS contain material with which children can practice their decoding skills independently of teacher direction. The decoding experiences thus provided increase the children's opportunities to discover sound-spelling relationships and to develop automatic word recognition. The workbooks are also an aid to vocabulary, word-meaning, and concept development, as they lead children to associate words with appropriate visual images and challenge children to deal with the meanings of words, phrases, and sentences. Finally, the workbooks are a useful tool with which to evaluate the children's decoding progress.

The workbook for Level C has nine sections of exercises, which correspond (in their sound-spelling patterns only) to the nine sections of the Level C reader, *Six Ducks in a Pond*. The exercises are not tied to the story content of the reader, however. Each section is identified by numbered tabs in the margins of its pages and begins with a word chart that presents most of the new words for that section of Level C. Each section progresses from simple exercises based on single words and phrases to more complex exercises involving phrases and sentences.

The workbook is easy to use. Children answer each item in one of three ways: by circling a word or phrase; by writing a numeral in a box; or by placing an X on a blank or in a circle. Since no handwriting skill is needed, the children's reading progress is kept independent of their handwriting progress. The reading lesson can proceed regardless of the children's handwriting abilities.

Some suggestions for the most effective use of the Level C workbook:

1. Do not ask the children to do the work in a given section of the workbook until they have become acquainted with the sound-spelling patterns used in that section. You may want to begin each section of the workbook by reading the word charts for that section with the children. Have the children read up and down the columns and across the rows, and discuss any unfamiliar words with them before proceeding to the exercises.

2. Throughout the first section of Level C, take care to see that each child understands the directions and is following them correctly before encouraging them to proceed on their own

3. If a child does not recognize a pictured object, simply tell them what it is.

4. Whenever possible, correct the children's work with them, reading the words, phrases, and sentences aloud and discussing the pictures. The more the children *hear* the words while looking at them, the greater will be their chance to develop automatic word recognition.

5. Try to assess the reasons for the children's errors and deal with them appropriately. Sometimes, as on the riddle pages, an error may be caused by faulty reasoning rather than by faulty decoding. At this stage, accurate decoding is a more important goal than perfect reasoning, and a child who decodes correctly but reasons poorly should still be praised for their reading.

6. Note that the "Yes or No" exercises are purposely written without clear-cut yes or no answers to every item. These pages should be discussed but not corrected. Make it a general rule *for all formats* not to put undue stress on getting the right answer. Instead, put the stress on accurate decoding and the enjoyment of using reading skills in a problem-solving situation.

Copyright © 2024, 2000, 1985, 1976, 1970, 1965, 1964 by the Estates of Donald E. Rasmussen and Lenina Goldberg. All rights reserved. Except as permitted under the United States Copyright Act, no part of this publication may be reproduced or distributed in any form or by any means, or stored in a database or retrieval system, without prior written permission from the publisher.

Email all inquiries to:
Peter Rasmussen, Editor
info@BasicReading.com

Website: BasicReading.com
ISBN 978-1-937547-03-5

_a_	_e_	_i_	_o_	_u_
	bell	Bill		
			doll	dull
	fell	fill		
		hill		hull
		Jill		
		kill		
		pill		
	sell	sill		
	tell	till		
	well	will		
	yell			
	Bess			
		kiss		
lass	less			
mass	mess	miss		muss
pass				
				cuff
				huff
	Jeff			
				puff
				buzz
		fizz		fuzz
add			odd	
	egg			
Ann		inn		

1

2

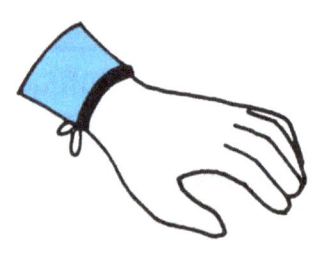
3

4

doll

bell

kiss

cuff

hill

Bess

egg

inn

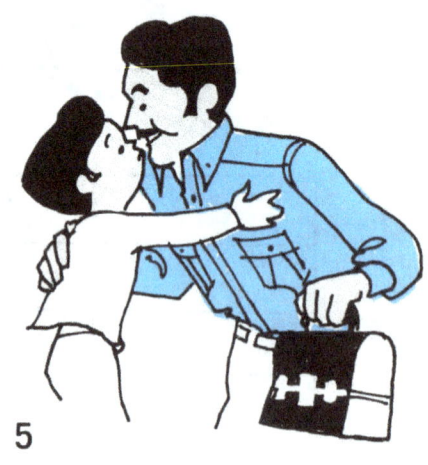
5

6

7

8

☒ fox on a hill
☐ bells in a box

☐ puff of a pig
☐ dots on a cuff

☐ Bess and a mess
☐ Bill has less

☐ fuzz on an egg
☐ buzz of a bug

☐ an egg in a pan
☐ the egg in a box

☐ Ann in the sun
☐ Bess on a bus

1

☐ Bill can fill it.
☐ Jill can tell it.

☐ Bill can tell.
☐ Bess can yell.

☐ Bess can tell it.
☐ Jill will sell it.

☐ Ann will add it.
☐ Bill will mess it up.

☐ The doll is well.
☐ The doll fell.

☐ Bess will kiss Mom.
☐ Jeff will miss Ann.

☒ The bus will pass.

☐ The bell will buzz.

☐ Miss Hill will tell.

☐ Jill is not well.

☐ The pig puffs.

☐ The pillbox fell.

☐ The inn is on a hill.

☐ Jill yells at Bill.

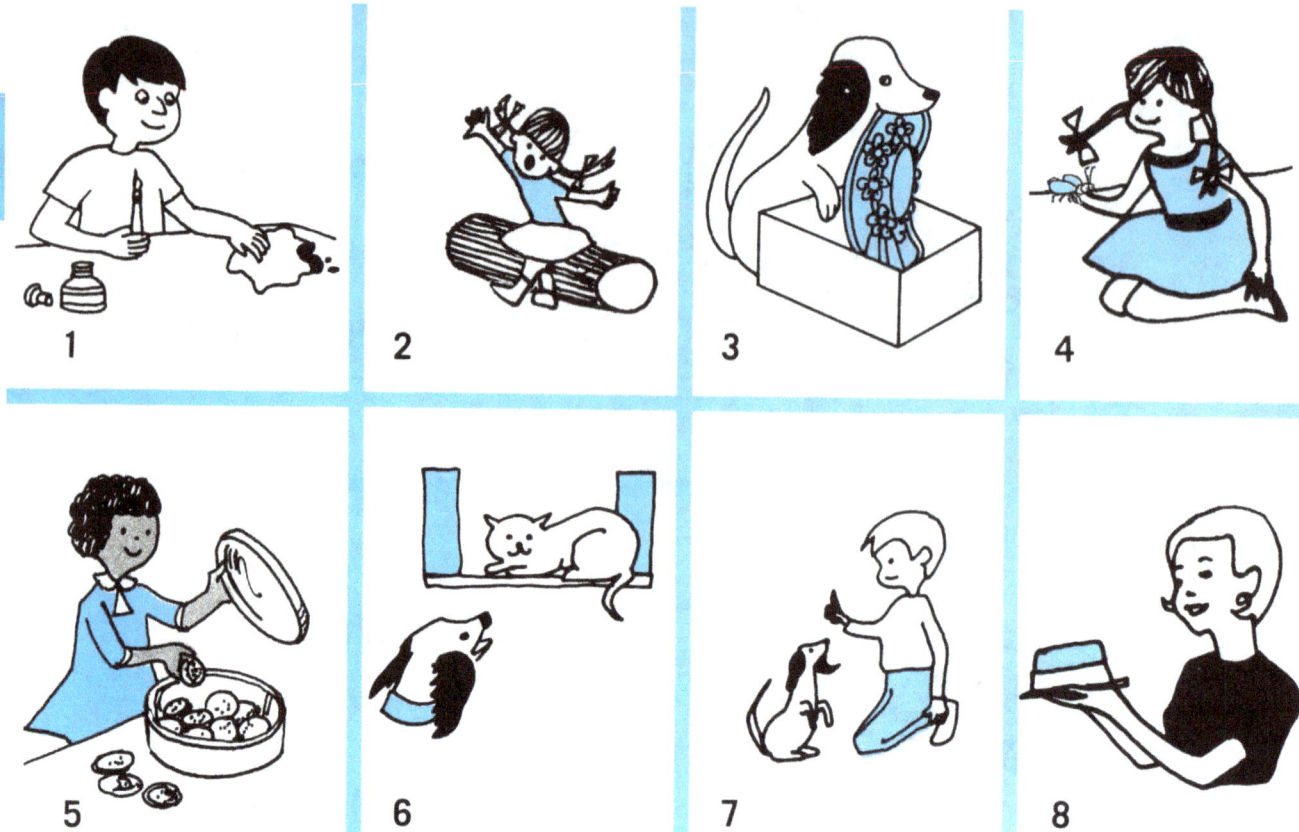

4	Bess will not kill the bug.
	Jill fills the tin box.
	Ann sits on the log and yells.
	Muff sits on the sill, and Ruff yells at him.
	Bill mops up his mess and fills his pen.
	Miss Hill sells hats to men.
	Ruff got Ann's hat and hid it in a box.
	Ben tells his pet to sit up and kiss him.

An egg fell on the rug.
Bess said, "I will mop up the

mass." (mess.") miss."

Bill's hat fell into the well.
Bill was upset and began to

yell. yet. yes.

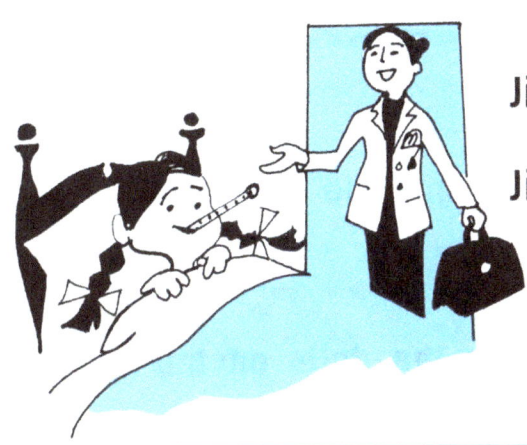

Jill fell and had to go to bed.
Jill was not

will. yell. well.

Tom said, "I will hit it.
It will go up to the top and hit the

bill." bell." bus."

1

☐ Ann fell and began to yell.

☐ Bess got up to kiss and hug Mom.

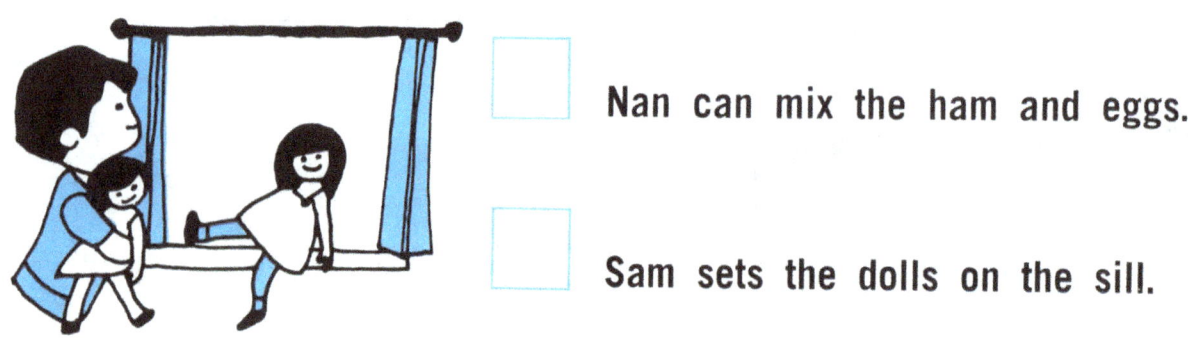

☐ Bill has a bug on his leg.

☐ Gus has six eggs to add to his box.

☐ Nan can mix the ham and eggs.

☐ Sam sets the dolls on the sill.

☐ Ted tells Wag to run.

☐ Ruff runs up the hill to the inn.

☐ The hen said, "I will sit on it.
But I will not let the man sell it."

☐ The fox said, "I will run up the hill.
And I will huff and puff till I get in."

☐ "A doll. A doll!" Bess had to yell.
Dad got a hug and a kiss.

☐ "I can tell it is a mess," said Jill.
"I will fix it up."

1

Bess and Bill at the well

	Yes	No
1. Will Bess add up a hill?	☐	☒
2. Will Bill fill up the jug in the well?	☐	☐
3. Will Bess get a doll to sit on the well?	☐	☐
4. Will Bess fill a cup at the well?	☐	☐
5. Will Bill get eggs in the well?	☐	☐
6. Will the sun set in the hills?	☐	☐
7. Will Bill sell eggs to Bess?	☐	☐

Dolls can nap in it.

The dolls can sit in it.

The top of it can go up.

It is a _____

A bell is in it.

The bell tells Dad to get up.

A six is on it.

It is a _____

Miss Hill can fix the hem on it.

And Bess can fix the cuffs.

It will fit Miss Hill.

It is a _____

_a_	_e_	_i_	_o_	_u_
back				
	deck	Dick	dock	duck
Jack				
		kick		
		lick	lock	luck
	neck	Nick		
pack	peck	pick		
		Rick	rock	
sack		sick	sock	suck
tack		tick		tuck

1

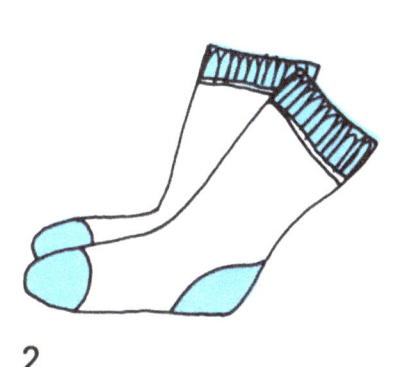
2

3

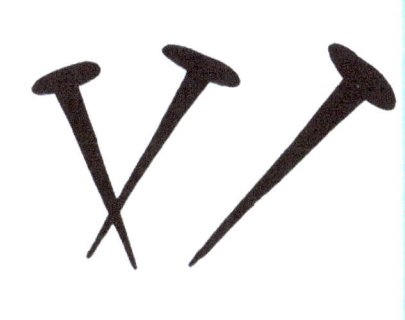
4

the rocks
the tacks
the duck
the sack
a neck
the lock
the dock
the socks

5

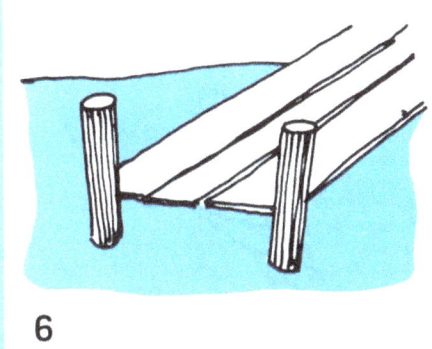
6

7

8

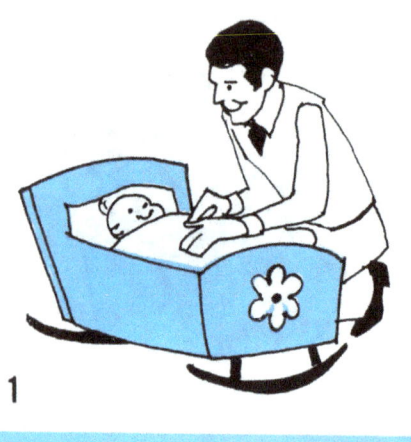

1

2

4

 Lick it.

Kick it.

 Pick it.

Dock it.

 Tack it.

Suck it.

 Lock it.

 Tuck it in.

5

6

7

8

☐ a duck on a rock
☐ a duck on a dock

☐ the back of a doll
☐ a pack on a duck

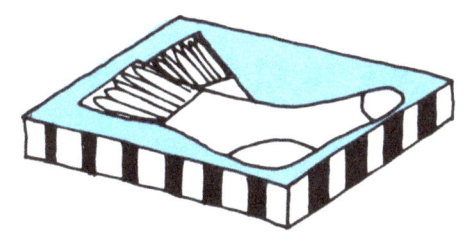

☐ the back of a fox
☐ the socks in a box

☐ a bag of tacks
☐ a box of pots

☐ ten locks on a box
☐ ten rocks on a hill

☐ a dog in a sack
☐ a leg in a sock

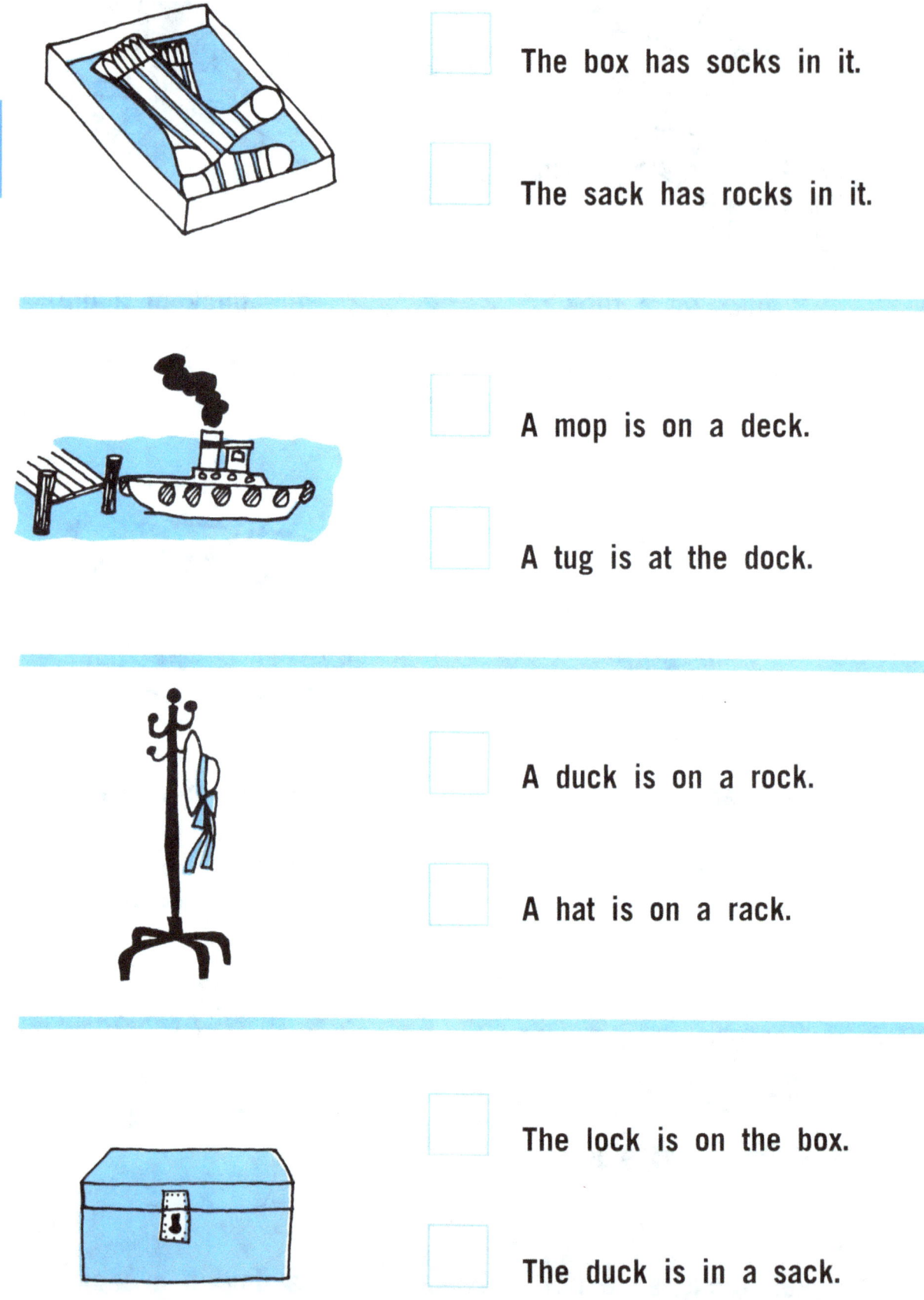

☐ The box has socks in it.

☐ The sack has rocks in it.

☐ A mop is on a deck.

☐ A tug is at the dock.

☐ A duck is on a rock.

☐ A hat is on a rack.

☐ The lock is on the box.

☐ The duck is in a sack.

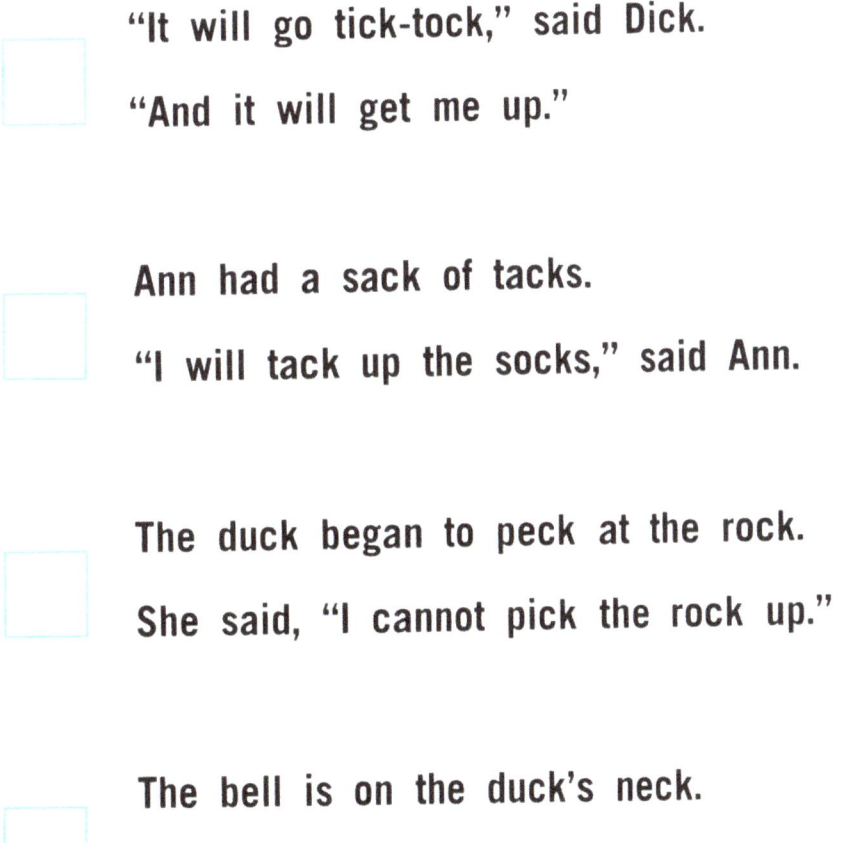

"It will go tick-tock," said Dick.
"And it will get me up."

Ann had a sack of tacks.
"I will tack up the socks," said Ann.

The duck began to peck at the rock.
She said, "I cannot pick the rock up."

The bell is on the duck's neck.
The duck said, "Jack will not miss me."

Jill ran up the hill.

She said, "I can get lots of rocks in my

sick." sack." suck."

Bill said, "I will tuck my cat in bed. My cat is

sock." suck." sick."

Miss Deck said, "I will pick up the sack. It will fit on my

pack." back." sock."

The man was on the deck.

He said, "I will get my tug to the

Dick." peck." dock."

☐ Dick began to pack his sack.

☐ Dick began to kick his sack.

2

☐ Ruff began to pick the duck's fuzz.

☐ The bug on Ruff's neck began to buzz.

☐ Mom began to mix up the tacks.

☐ Mom began to pick up the duck.

☐ Kit will lick up the mess.

☐ Dick will lock up the mess.

2

Ann and Jack on a dock

	Yes	No
1. Jack yells to a man on the deck.		
2. Six ducks sit on the rocks to nap.		
3. A pack is on Jack's back.		
4. Ann and Jack sit back to back on the dock.		
5. A sack is on the dock.		
6. A duck picks up a bug in its bill.		
7. Ann has no socks on.		

I can rock it.

I can tuck it in bed.

I can hug it.

It is a ☐ ☐ ☐

A sock fits on it.

It can kick.

A duck can peck at it.

 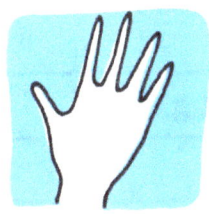 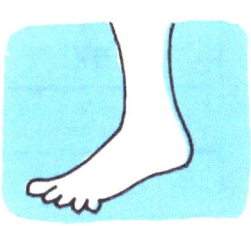

It is a ☐ ☐ ☐

I can pick it up.

It can hit tacks.

It cannot go tick-tock.

It is a ☐ ☐ ☐

_a_	_e_	_i_	_o_	_u_
and	end			
band	bend			
			fond	
hand				
land	lend			
	mend			
			pond	
sand	send			
		wind		
ant				
	bent			
can't				
	dent			
		hint		hunt
	lent			
		mint		
pants				
	rent			
	sent			
	tent	tint		
	went			

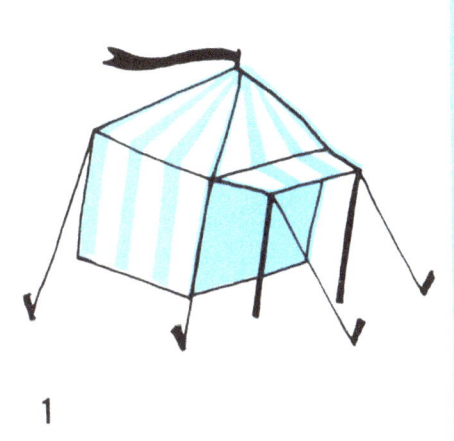
1

2

3

4

a pond

a hand

a band

Bill's pants

an ant

a tent

the wind

the sand

5

6

7

8

3

- [ ] a man in the pond
- [ ] a man in the wind

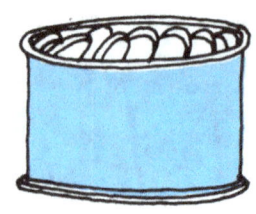

- [ ] the mints in a can
- [ ] the mend in the pants

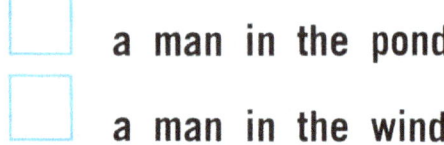

- [ ] the ducks on a pond
- [ ] the sand in the pond

- [ ] the tents on the sand
- [ ] the eggs in the tent

- [ ] the cuffs on his pants
- [ ] the rocks in his packs

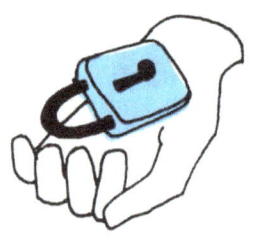

- [ ] a rock in a pond
- [ ] a lock in a hand

☐ Ann went up the hill.

☐ Ann went into the pond.

☐ Jack sent the doll to Jeff.

☐ Jill lent the box to Bess.

☐ Dad has to mend his pants.

☐ Mr. Hill has to land the jet.

☐ Dad put up the tent.

☐ Dad put the sand into the sandbox.

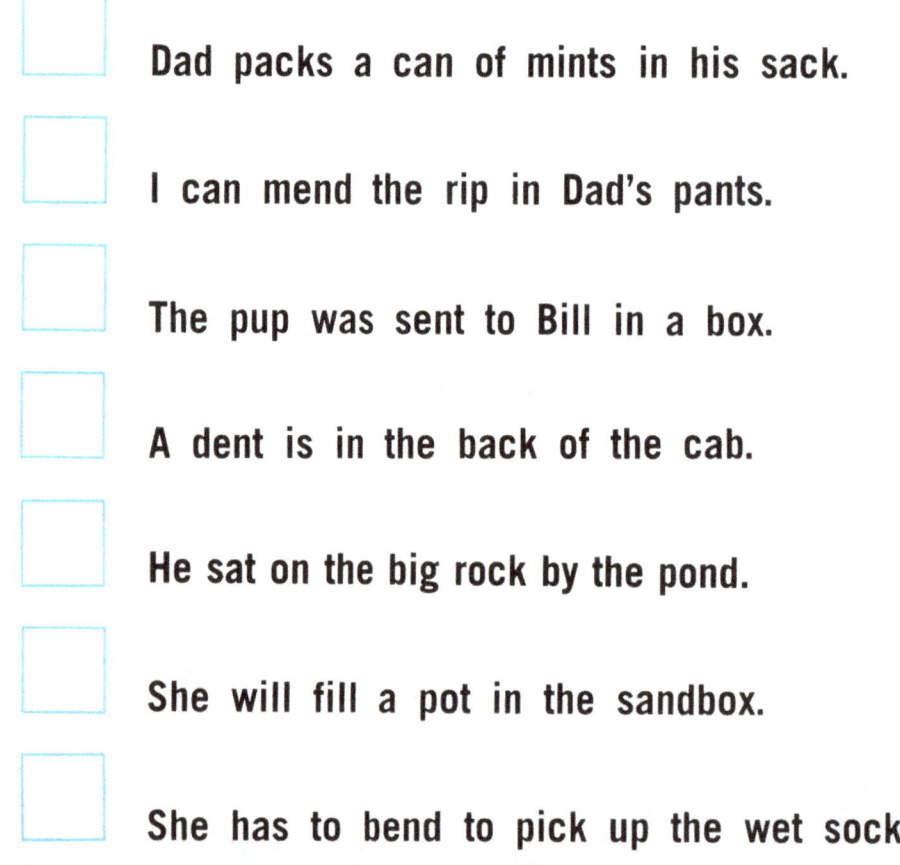

- Dad packs a can of mints in his sack.
- I can mend the rip in Dad's pants.
- The pup was sent to Bill in a box.
- A dent is in the back of the cab.
- He sat on the big rock by the pond.
- She will fill a pot in the sandbox.
- She has to bend to pick up the wet socks.
- He will get his tug to the dock in the wind.

Mrs. Jacks went up the hill.
She said, "I will set up a

tint."   bent."   tent."

Bess has six ants.
She said, "I will let the ants run in the

sand."   send."   sent."

Ann and Jack sat in the tent.
Ann said, "I will lend Jack my

sands."   socks."   sacks."

Mr. Hunt was upset. He said,
"I can't get the tug back to the

duck."   dent."   dock."

Yes and No

An ant is a bug,

    but can it hug?

Yes____   No____

Jack can dig in the sand,

    but can he pick it up in his hand?

Yes____   No____

Ann Hunt can mend a dent,

    but can she rent a tent?

Yes____   No____

Sand can get wet,

    but can it get set?

Yes____   No____

1

2

3

4

"I will put it in my sandbox," said Jill.
"It will be fun in the sand."

Ann sat by the pond. She said,
"The wind sent it into my hand."

"I am fond of the pond," said the duck.
"But my pal can't go in."

"The wind got my hat," said Mrs. Hill.
"But I can get it back."

A Jack-in-the-box is fun.

	Yes	No
1. The jack-in-the-box has bells on his cap.	☐	☐
2. He has big cuffs on his pants.	☐	☐
3. A lock is on the lid of the box.	☐	☐
4. He has a sack in his hand.	☐	☐
5. He can put on his pants.	☐	☐
6. He can run, but he can't kick.	☐	☐
7. Jack can bend in his box.	☐	☐

It can be tan.

I can nap in it.

A puff of wind can rip it.

Is it
- a band
- (a tent)
- a dent

It can be a pet.

It gets wet in the pond.

It is not upset if it gets wet.

Is it
- a handbag
- a neck
- a duck

It can huff and puff.

It can pick up sand.

It can send a man's hat up a hill.

Is it
- the land
- the rent
- the wind

-a-	-e-	-i-	-o-	-u-
	best			
				dust
fast		fist		
				just
last		list		
		mist		must
	nest			
past	pest			
	rest			rust
	test			
	vest			
	west			
ask				
	desk			dusk
				husk
mask				
task				tusk

1

2

3

4

a mask ☐

a nest ☐

a vest ☐

a fist ☐

a list ☐

a rest ☐

a desk ☐

a pest ☐

5

6

7

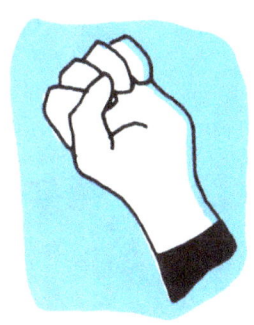

8

4

- [ ] eggs in a nest
- [ ] wind in the west

- [ ] a pest in a tent
- [ ] a rest on a cot

- [ ] a pen on a desk
- [ ] a dent in a tusk

- [ ] ants in the dust
- [ ] pants and a vest

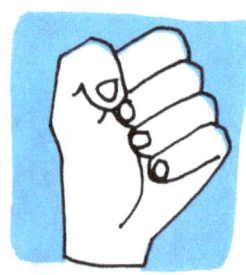

- [ ] a hint on the list
- [ ] a hand in a fist

- [ ] a mask on a doll
- [ ] mist on a hill

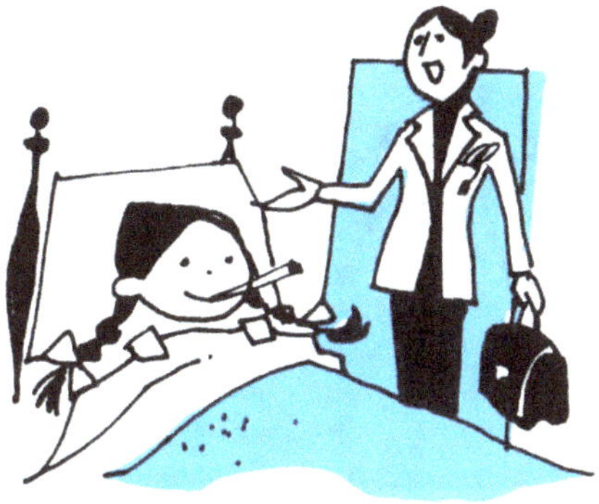

☐ You must rest in bed.

☐ You must dust the bed.

☐ He must list it last.

☐ He just got set to go.

☐ Dad has on his best vest.

☐ Dad runs into the west wind.

☐ The sun sets in the west.

☐ The ant sits and rests.

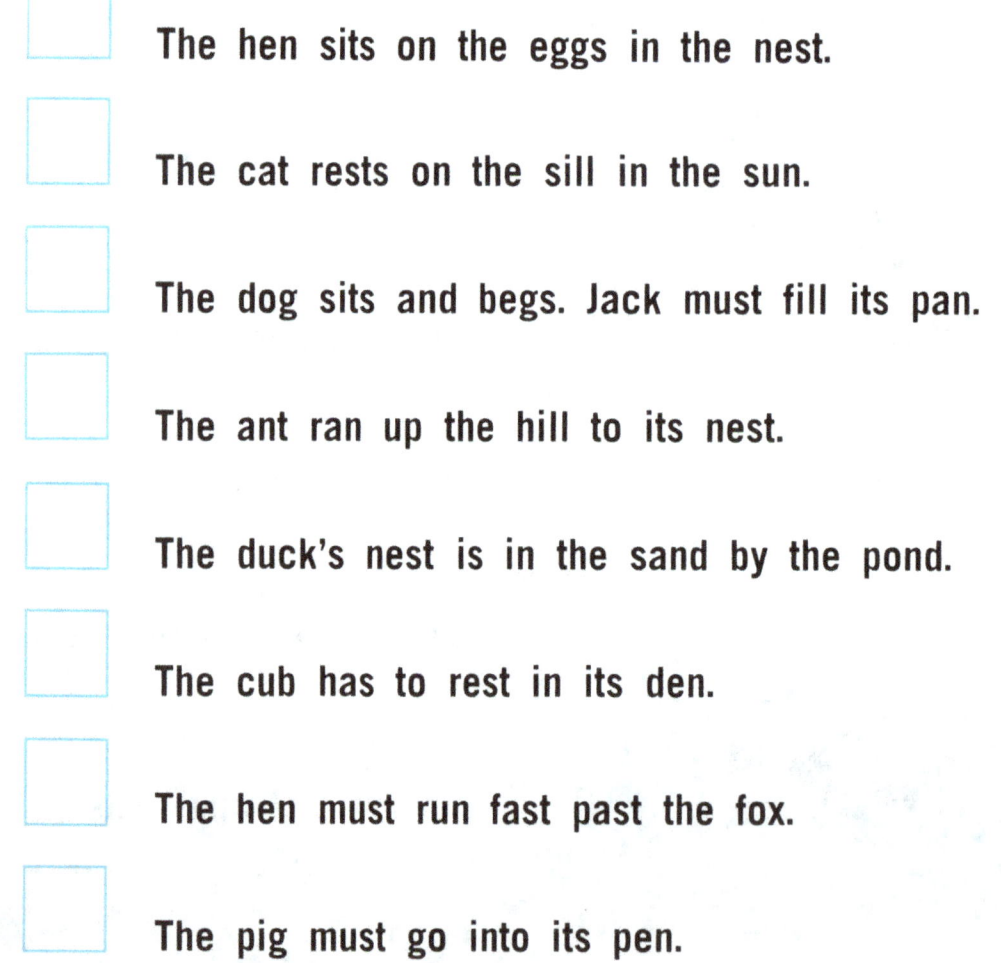

☐ The hen sits on the eggs in the nest.

☐ The cat rests on the sill in the sun.

☐ The dog sits and begs. Jack must fill its pan.

☐ The ant ran up the hill to its nest.

☐ The duck's nest is in the sand by the pond.

☐ The cub has to rest in its den.

☐ The hen must run fast past the fox.

☐ The pig must go into its pen.

Dick had a box in his hand.
He said, "I must put eggs on my

lent." last." list."

Jack said, "I will have fun."
He asks, "Mom, can I have the

mist?" mask?" must?"

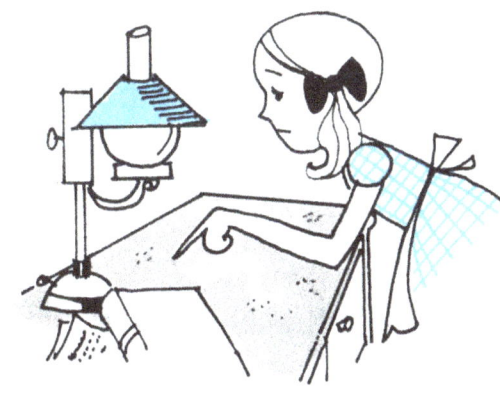

Lots of dust is on the desk.
Ann asks, "Will Dad dust his

task?" desk?" disk?"

Bess ran and ran up the hill.
She said, "I will be last. I must run

fast." fist." fill."

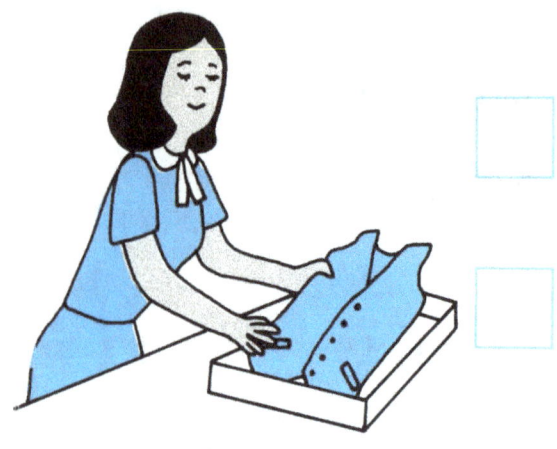

☐ Mom put Jack's vest into a box.

☐ Mom put Jack's test on his desk.

4

☐ Jack has ten sums to add at his desk.

☐ Rick must put on his best socks.

☐ The duck's nest is in the sand by the pond.

☐ The duck ran past the last nest.

☐ Ann's fist hit the bag, and the eggs fell.

☐ Ann's mask has dots and a net on it.

1

2

3

4

☐ "You can pet it," said Jill.
"It will not peck you."

☐ "It is a big job.
I must have a rest," said Dad.

☐ You can put it on the rug, and
it will suck up the dust.

☐ "It will rust if it gets wet.
I must put it in a box," said Miss West.

Jack's pals at the desks

Bess   Jim   Jack   Ann

	Yes	No
1. Jack has a pen and a test on his desk.	☐	☐
2. Jack's desk has a bent leg.	☐	☐
3. Jim's hand is up. He has a lot to ask.	☐	☐
4. Jim has dustrags he must pick up.	☐	☐
5. Bess must mend the tent.	☐	☐
6. Bess sits in back of Jack and Jim.	☐	☐
7. Ann has a doll on top of the desk.	☐	☐

It is tan and big.

You can dust and wax it.

It has a pen and a pad on it.

Is it — a mask
— a desk
— a task

4

I pick it up.

I put it in my handbag.

It tells me I must get eggs.

Is it — a fist
— a test
— a list

It can be red.

Dad puts it on.

It fits him well.

Is it — a task
— a vest
— a gust

_a_	_e_	_i_	_o_	_u_
				bump
camp				
damp				dump
				hump
				jump
lamp				lump
				pump
		gift		
	left	lift		
raft				
		sift		
act				
	kept			
	wept			
	next			
	elf			
	self			
		milk		
		silk		
	help			
	yelp			
	held			
	belt			
	felt			
	melt			

1

2

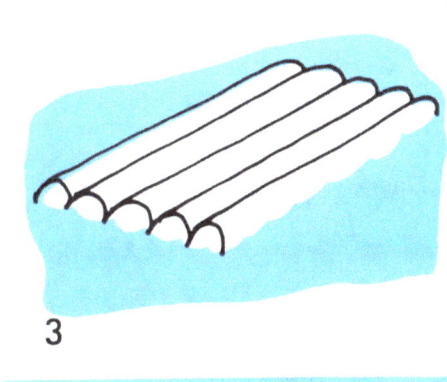
3

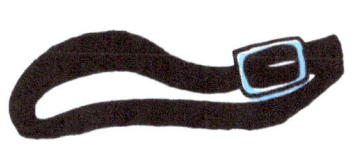
4

a lamp ☐

a belt ☐

a gift ☐

a raft ☐

a camp ☐

an elf ☐

a pump ☐

the milk ☐

5

6

7

8

5

- [ ] the best lamp
- [ ] the damp land

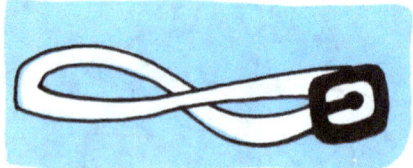

- [ ] the next bump
- [ ] the silk belt

- [ ] the milkman's milk
- [ ] the milkman's mint

- [ ] the last egg
- [ ] the fast elf

- [ ] the elf left
- [ ] the best gifts

- [ ] the silk vest
- [ ] the camp pest

☐ It melts in the sun.

☐ The milk is in the cup.

☐ Mrs. West left the raft.

☐ Mrs. West can lift the gift.

☐ The elf can jump by itself.

☐ The ant can rest by itself.

☐ The milk helps the elf.

☐ The elf held the milk.

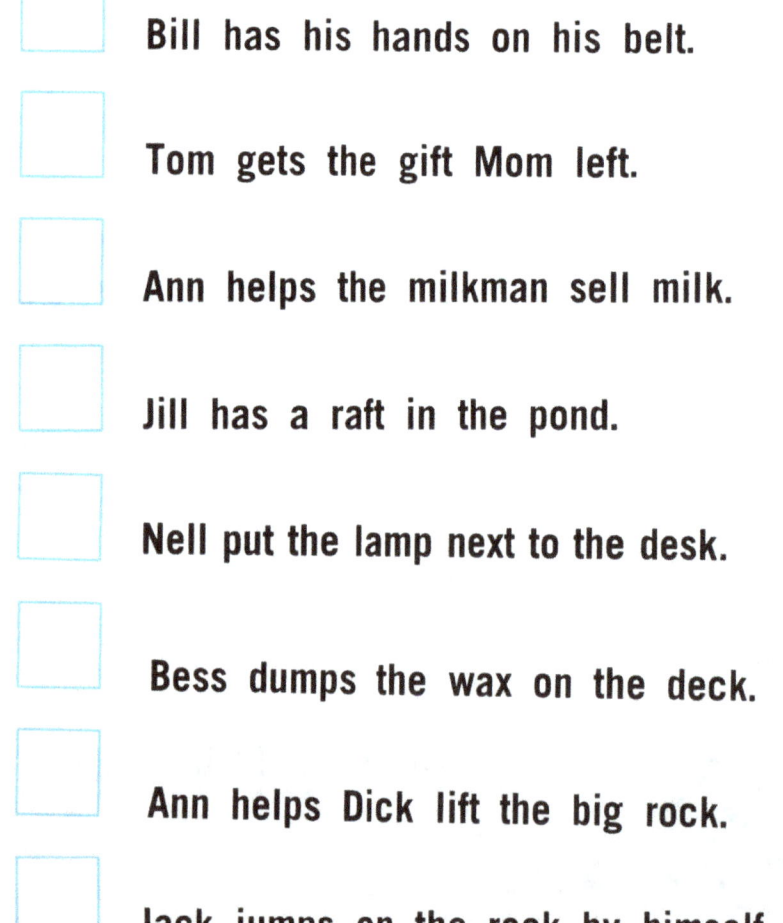

☐ Bill has his hands on his belt.

☐ Tom gets the gift Mom left.

☐ Ann helps the milkman sell milk.

☐ Jill has a raft in the pond.

☐ Nell put the lamp next to the desk.

☐ Bess dumps the wax on the deck.

☐ Ann helps Dick lift the big rock.

☐ Jack jumps on the rock by himself.

Bill said, "Let me help, Mom.
We could melt it in the

pump."   gift."   pot."

Jack said, "I must put it in the tent.
I could lift it if I had

held."   hump."   help."

5

Dad said, "I must get rid of the lumps.
I could sift the mix into a

cup."   gift."   camp."

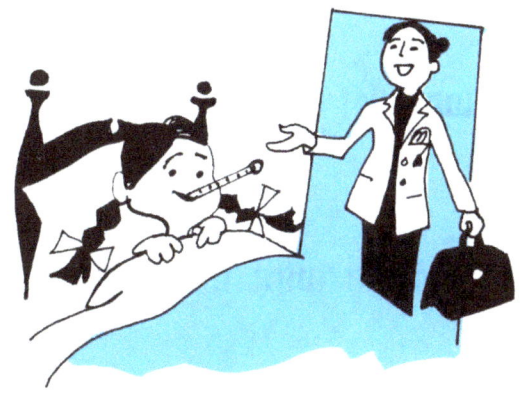

Doc West said to Bess, "You must rest.
You have the

masks."   humps."   mumps."

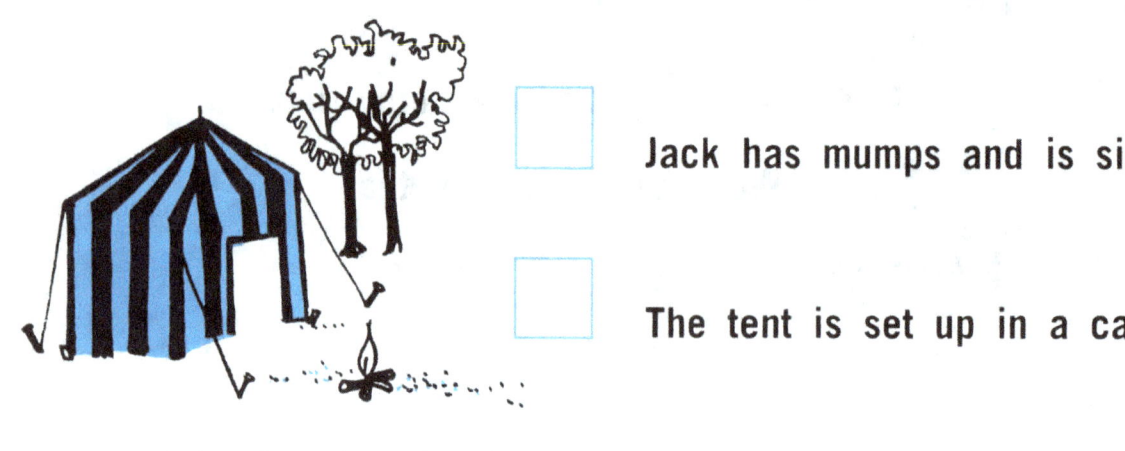

☐ Jack has mumps and is sick in bed.

☐ The tent is set up in a camp.

☐ Gus hit the bug on his left leg.

☐ Jack was next to the last on the raft.

☐ Jack could not win, so he wept.

☐ If Jack could jump up, he would win.

☐ Dick held a lump of wax in his hand.

☐ Dick did not have a mint in his hand.

Yes and No

She can lift a lamp,

but can she lift a camp?

Yes____   No____

An elf can jump,

but can he pump?

Yes____   No____

A man can help an elf,

but can he help himself?

Yes____   No____

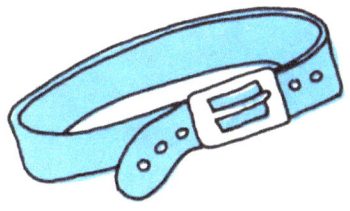

A belt can be silk,

but can it sip milk?

Yes____   No____

The men in the West

	Yes	No
1. The men have mumps and must rest.	☐	☐
2. A man has a bun in his hand.	☐	☐
3. A man has his hand on a silk neck band.	☐	☐
4. A man jumps off a raft into a pond.	☐	☐
5. The man fell off the rock and wept.	☐	☐
6. The men have belts on.	☐	☐
7. The man on the left has a lamp in his hand.	☐	☐

It can jump and buzz.

It can land on you.

It can be a pest in camp.

Is it — an egg

Is it — a bug

— an elf

It can be kept in a jug.

The milkman can lift it.

Pups and cats lap it up.

Is it — the land

Is it — the mist

— the milk

It was a gift.

Tom put it on by himself.

It kept Tom's pants up.

Is it — a belt

Is it — a bump

— a lamp

5

-a-	-e-	-i-	-o-	-u-
	bled			
				club
clam				
clap		clip		
	fled			
flag				
flap		flip	flop	
flat		flit		
glad				
	Glen			
				plug
				plum
plan				
				plus
	sled	slid		
slam		slim		
slap		slip	slop	
		slit	slot	

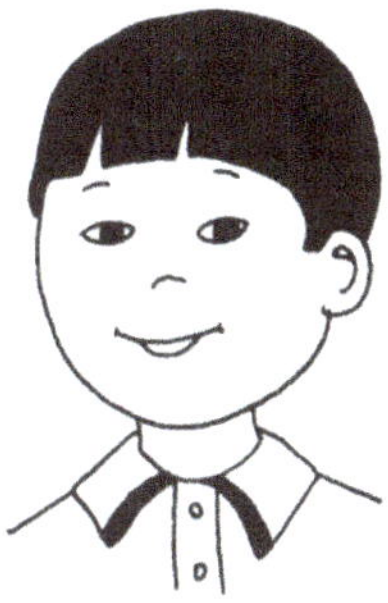

1

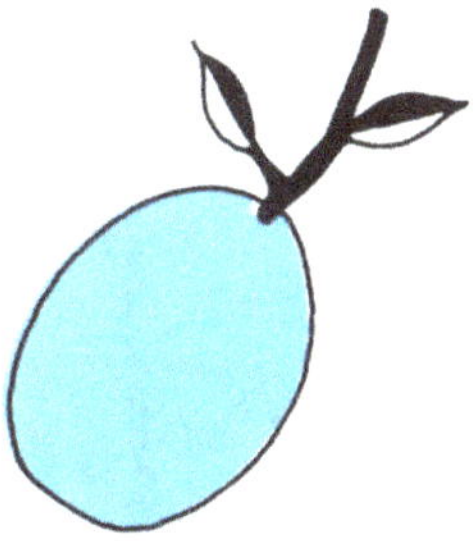

2

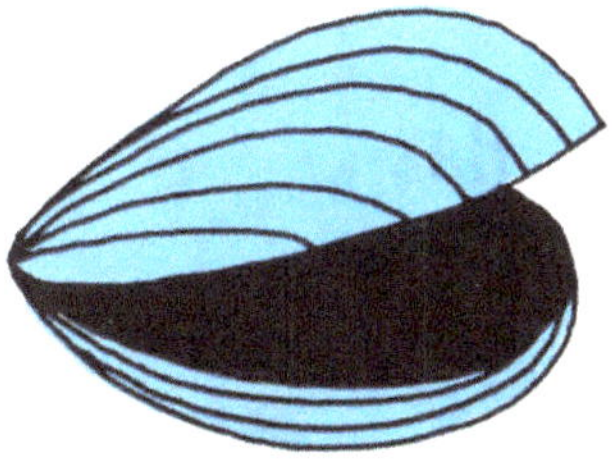

3

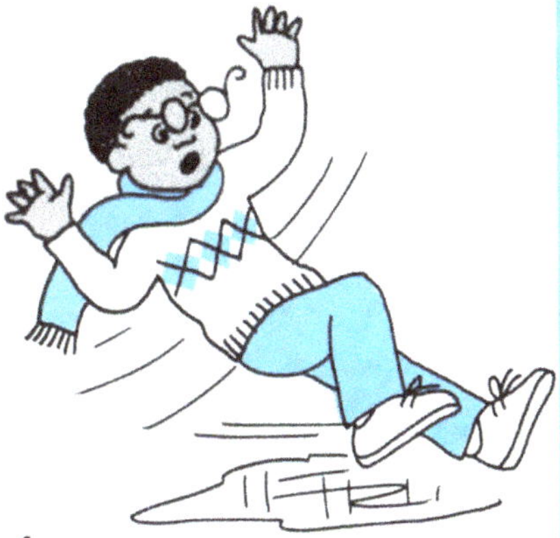

4

a sled

to slip

a clip

a clam

a club

a plum

a flag

Glen

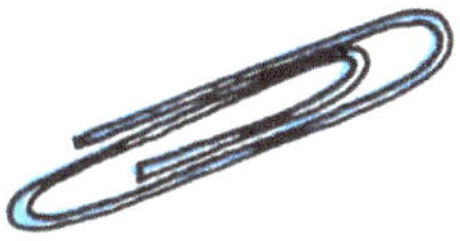

5

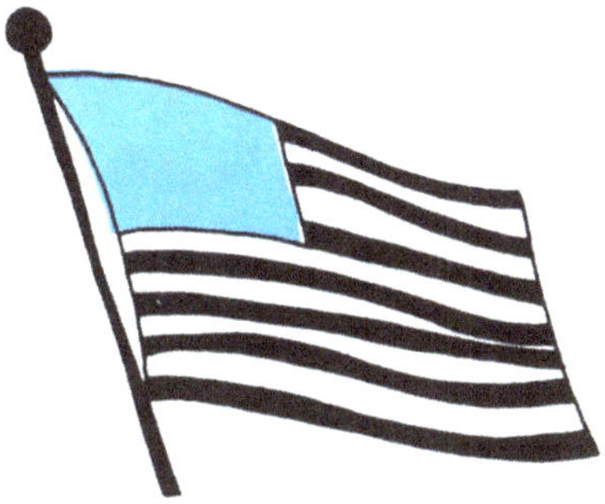

6

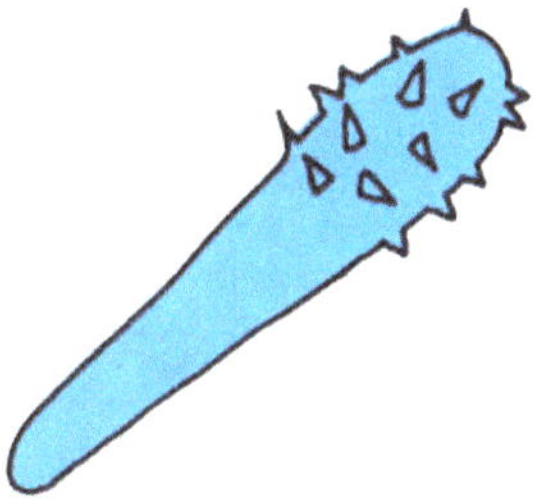

7

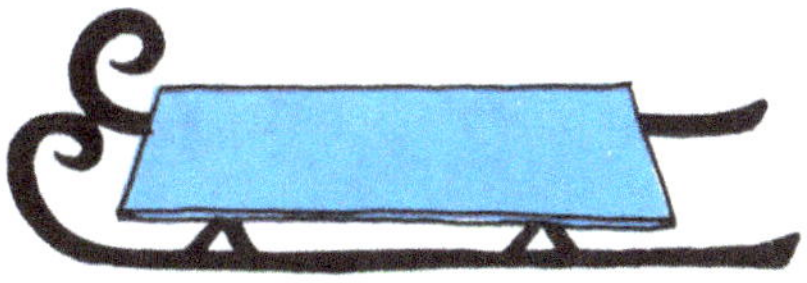

8

6

☐ 6
+10

☐ a six plus ten
☐ a set of plans

☐ A sled can slap.
☐ A sled can slip.

☐ Bess can clap.
☐ Gus can clip it.

☐ The map is flat.
☐ The flag can flap.

☐ Bill has a gift.
☐ Bill has a club.

☐ Glen can flop on it.
☐ Glen can flap at it.

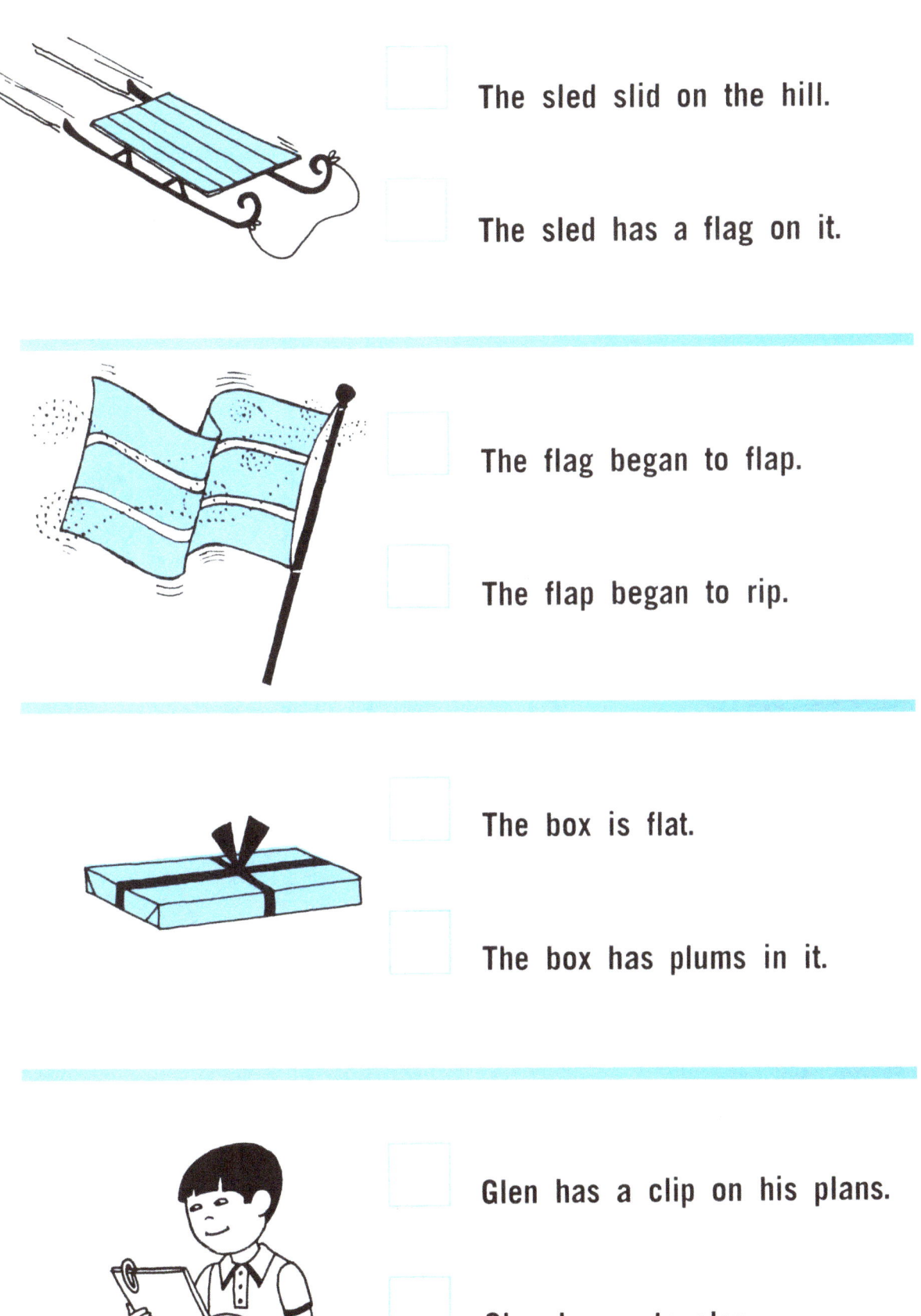

☐ The sled slid on the hill.

☐ The sled has a flag on it.

☐ The flag began to flap.

☐ The flap began to rip.

☐ The box is flat.

☐ The box has plums in it.

☐ Glen has a clip on his plans.

☐ Glen began to clap.

1

3

4

6

 6

☐ Jill held the flag on the raft.

☐ Glen jumps and flops on the mat.

☐ Glen has plums in his sack.

☐ Glen slid on his red sled.

☐ Ann held the club in her hand.

☐ Miss Will puts the pen and clips on the desk.

Jill said, "Let's have fun.
Let's flop on your

    slip."   slid."   sled."

Ann said, "I can't tell what you have in the pot."
Dad said, "They are

    claps."   clams."   clips."

Tom said, "We have to get a tent.
If we have a tent, we can have a

    club."   clip."   clam."

Jill said, "Let's have a club.
I will tell you my

    plums."   plans."   plus."

☐ Glen flops on his bed to rest.

☐ Glen is glad to have the flag.

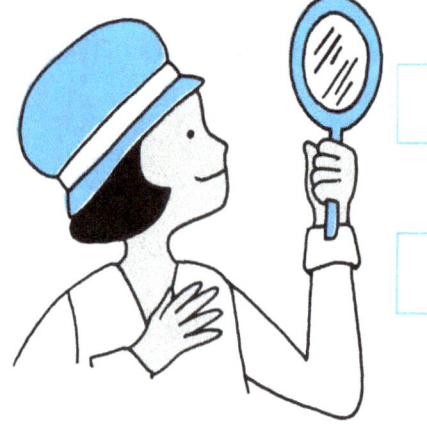

☐ Mom puts on her best silk hat.

☐ Mom is glad to have a plan.

☐ Ann has to slam the box to lock it.

☐ Ann claps. She is glad to have a mask.

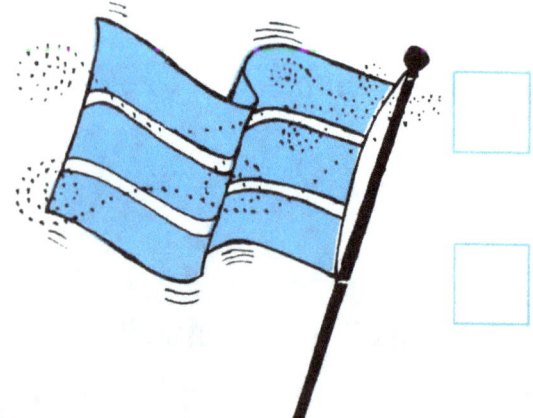

☐ The flag flaps in the wind.

☐ The flag is in a flat box.

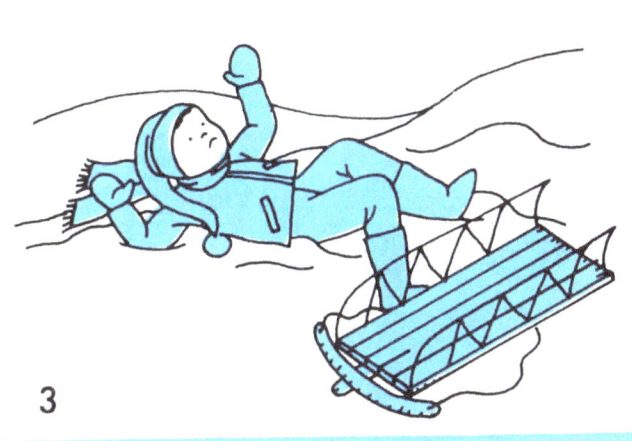

Jill said, "I will get in bed.
But I will not flip and flop on it."

Bill said, "My sled slid on the hill.
It hit a bump and I fell off."

Miss Hunt asks Glen, "What is six plus six? Can you add it?"

Jack sent a big box to Ann.
Ann asks, "What is in it?"

A club on the hill

Jack   Glen   Jill

6

	Yes	No

1. Jack bends to get into the tent.

2. They have a tent set up on the hill.

3. Glen put up a flag by the tent.

4. Jack put a plum on the tent flap.

5. Glen is glad they have a club.

6. "The Best Club" is on the flag.

7. Jill hits the pegs to put up the tent.

It can clip.

It can cut.

It must not slip.

It is a   ☐

The wind can slam it.

Dad can lock it.

It is flat.

It is a ☐ ☐ ☐

You can add it.

It has a plus.

It can be on your test.

It is a ☐ ☐ ☐

_a_	_e_	_i_	_o_	_u_
		skid		
		skin		
		skip		
		skit		
snag				snug
snap		snip		
	sped			
		spin		spun
spat		spit	spot	
stab				stub
	stem			
Stan				
	step		stop	
swam		swim		swum
		twig		
		twin		

1

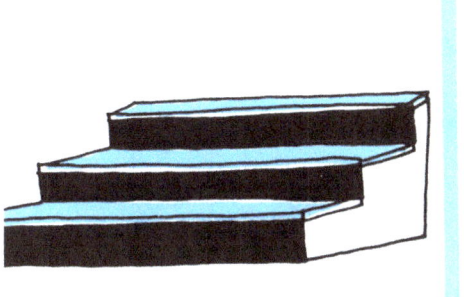
2

3

4

steps
swims
twins
spins
spots
skips
twigs
skids

5

6

7

8

☐ step of a hut
☐ stem of a bud

☐ stop for a swim
☐ step up to win

☐ sun in the west
☐ snug in a nest

☐ clams in a tub
☐ clips in a box

☐ stem on a plum
☐ steps to a club

☐ a nest of twigs
☐ spots on the skin

☐ A stem can bend.
☐ A twig can spin.

☐ A sled can stop.
☐ A top can spin.

☐ Jack can skip.
☐ Dad can snip.

☐ A duck can swim.
☐ A step can slip.

☐ Scot swims in the tub.
☐ Stan spins the top.

☐ To swim is fun.
☐ To skip is fun.

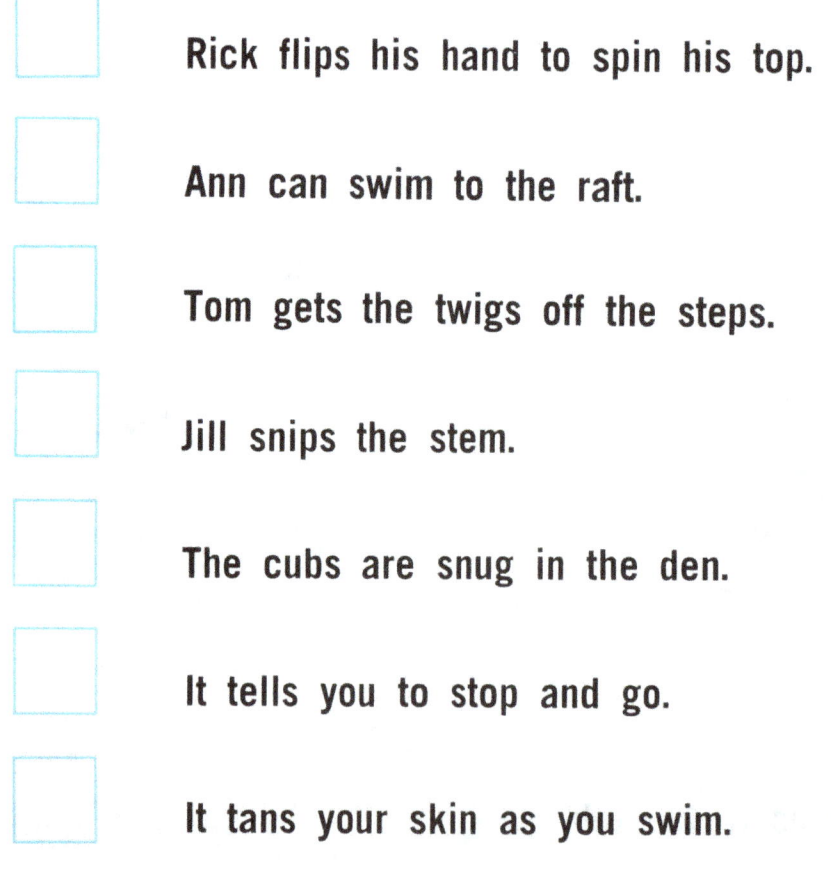

7

☐ Rick flips his hand to spin his top.

☐ Ann can swim to the raft.

☐ Tom gets the twigs off the steps.

☐ Jill snips the stem.

☐ The cubs are snug in the den.

☐ It tells you to stop and go.

☐ It tans your skin as you swim.

☐ Bess skids to a stop.

"I know Bill can act," said Stan.
"I will ask him to help me put on a

skip."   skit."   swim."

Six ducks went to the pond for a swim.
Mom Duck asks, "Did you swim at the pond?"
They tell her, "Yes, we

skim."   spun."   swam."

Dad got a gift for Ann. Ann's dad said,
"It is a top. If you flip it fast, it will

span."   spin."   spun."

Jill fell and got a cut on the hand.
"Bad luck!" she said, "I will get a big

skit."   scab."   snub."

☐ Stan can skip as fast as the wind.

☐ Spot went into the pond for a swim.

☐ The milkman left the milk on the steps.

☐ The twins help the milkman with his job.

☐ Scot's raft has a tent on it.

☐ Ann swam to the raft.

☐ Glen felt the twig snap.

☐ Glen felt spots on his fist.

The rug was a mess. Stan felt sad.

Stan said, "I can help.

I will help get the spots off the rug."

Snip! Snap! went the duck.

"Stop!" said Nell. "If you snap at me,

I will not swim in your pond."

A fat duck sat on a nest.

She said, "You cannot have my eggs.

I will stop you."

Stan could run, but he could not skip.

Jill said, "Stan, I will help you skip.

Just hop and step." And Stan did.

Yes and No

A top can spin,

    but can it swim?

Yes____   No____

A cab can skid,

    but can it skip?

Yes____   No____

A twig can snap,

    but can it map?

Yes____   No____

A flag can flap,

    but can it clap?

Yes____   No____

Jill and Bill at the pond

	Yes	No
1. The twins are at the pond for a swim.	☐	☐
2. Jill put the sand in her cuff.	☐	☐
3. Bill got six clams.	☐	☐
4. Jill put the clams in a sack.	☐	☐
5. Jill has a flag on the top of the hill.	☐	☐
6. The twins can swim in the sand.	☐	☐
7. Bill let the clams snap at the flag.	☐	☐

If Stan bends it, it will snap.

It can be cut and put into a box.

It is not a log.

Is it
- a twig
- a twin
- a skin

It can be on a dog's back.

You can get it on a vest.

You must rub it to get rid of it.

Is it
- a stop
- a slot
- a spot

If you swim, it gets wet.

It can get hot.

It can get cut.

Is it
- a skip
- a skit
- skin

_a_	_e_	_i_	_o_	_u_
Brad				
brag				
		brim		
crab		crib		
			crop	
drag				drug
				drum
		drip	drop	
	Fred			
			frog	
Fran				
grab				
		grin		
		grip		
		trim		
trap		trip		
			trot	

1

2

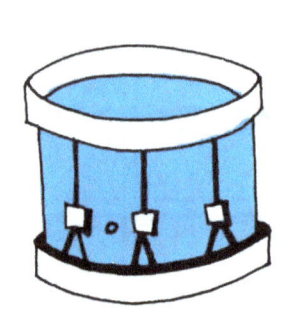
3

4

crab

crib

frog

drum

to drag

to drip

to trim

to grab

5

6

7

8

☐ fox in a trap
☐ frog in a pond

☐ Fred in a crib
☐ flag on a sled

☐ plum on a twig
☐ plug on a lamp

☐ trim of a vest
☐ brim of a hat

☐ drip a drop
☐ drop an egg

☐ A trip can end.
☐ A twig can bend.

☐ A crab can snap.
☐ Brad can brag.

☐ Fred can trot.
☐ Stan can spot.

☐ A frog can flop.
☐ A flag can flap.

☐ Mom can trim.
☐ Fran can grin.

☐ A drum can be hit.
☐ A drop can be hot.

☐ Ann has a trip.
☐ Ann has a trap.

☐ Fred got the trap.

☐ Fran hit the drum.

☐ Brad set a trap to get a fox.

☐ Jill went on a trip to get the flags.

☐ The two crabs were in the trap.

☐ The two cribs were for the twins.

☐ Stan let his wet hands drip on his vest.

☐ Dick let the wet sand drip in the nest.

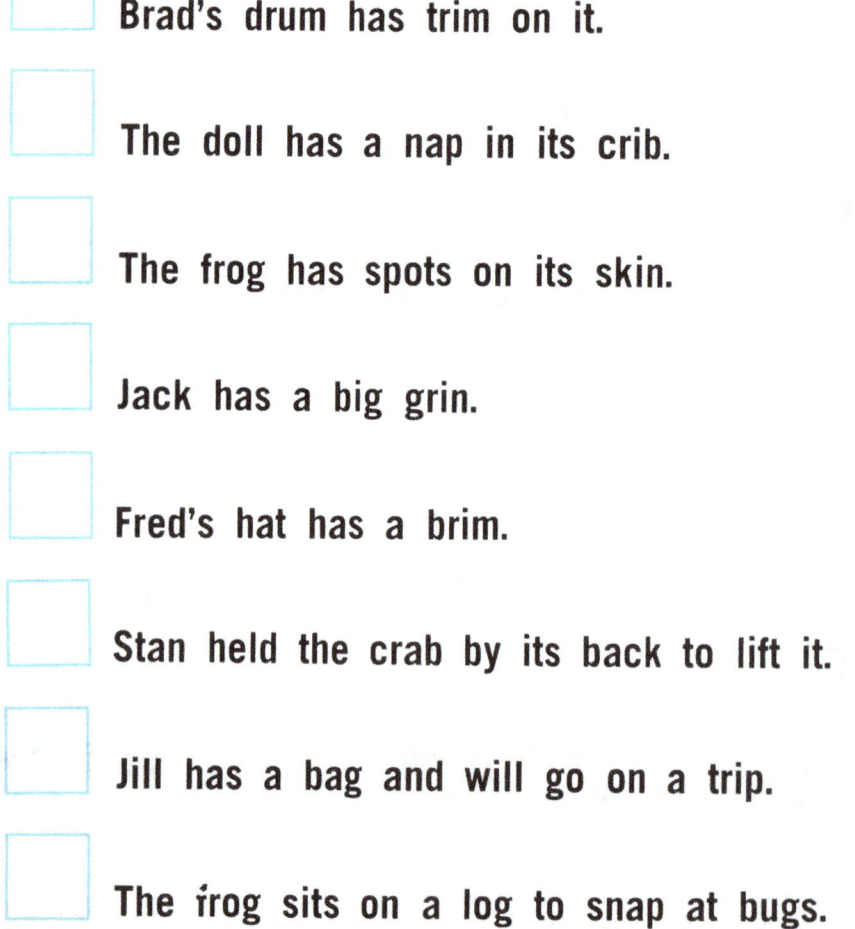

☐ Brad's drum has trim on it.

☐ The doll has a nap in its crib.

☐ The frog has spots on its skin.

☐ Jack has a big grin.

☐ Fred's hat has a brim.

☐ Stan held the crab by its back to lift it.

☐ Jill has a bag and will go on a trip.

☐ The frog sits on a log to snap at bugs.

Stan got his hand on the frog, but it swam off. The frog said, "You can't grab me. I can slip from your

grim." grin." grip."

If your doll wants to rest, you should put it in a

crab. crib. crop.

Fran did not know what to do next. She said, "What a mess! I am in a

trip." trap." trot."

Brad said, "I can swim as fast as any frog." Brad could

brag! crag! brig!

☐ Fran trims a hat for Mom.

☐ Fran trips on the flat rock.

☐ Stan wants to grab Don's milk.

☐ Stan was glad to have the drum.

☐ Two clams dug into the wet sand.

☐ The crabs swam from the dock.

☐ The frog has two spots on its skin.

☐ Bugs go by and frogs snap at them.

1   2   3   4

☐ Jim said to Fran, "Ask Dad to let us go on a trip to trap frogs."

Fran said, "Ask Dad yourself, Jim. I will not help you trap frogs. They should be kept in the pond."

☐ Fran said, "Mom, what can I do to help you?"

Mom said, "You can drag that log off the steps."

☐ "It is fun to have a drum," said Jim.

"You can slap it and hit it, and it will not hit you back."

☐ "You have many pills and drugs," said Jack.

"What are they for?"

"They can help you get well," said the man.

"But you should not have any if you are not sick."

Will you grin?

Bill　　　Bess　　　Jim　　　Ann

If you trip Bess, will she grin?

　　　Yes____　　　No____

If Ann grabs a plum and drops it, will she grin?

　　　Yes____　　　No____

If a crab grabs Jim, will he grin?

　　　Yes____　　　No____

If Bill gets a frog, will he grin?

　　　Yes____　　　No____

If you grab it, it will snap at you.

It has legs, but it cannot run fast.

You can trap it and sell it.

Is it
- a grab
- a crab
- a crib

It hops and can have spots.

It can swim fast.

It sits on a log to sun itself.

Is it
- a grab
- a frog
- a band

It has skin, but no hands or legs.

You can hit it, but it will not yell.

It is in a band.

Is it
- a drug
- a drum
- a drag

-a-	-e-	-i-	-o-	-u-
		cliff		
				gruff
		sniff		
staff		stiff		stuff
		drill		
	smell			
	spell	spill		
		still		
	swell			
	bless			
class				
	dress			
glass				
grass				
	press			
black			block	
		brick		
		click	clock	
crack				
		flick	flock	
smack				
snack				
stack		stick	stock	stuck
track		trick		truck

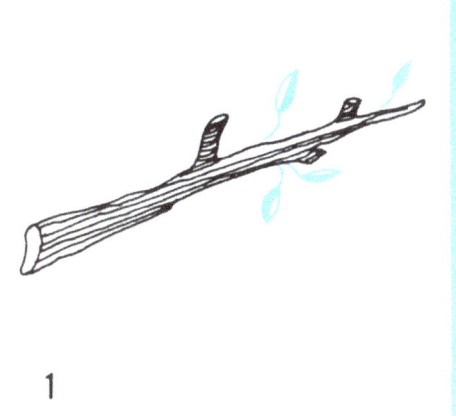

1

2

3

4

a truck

a trick

a brick

a stick

a clock

the grass

a glass

a dress

5

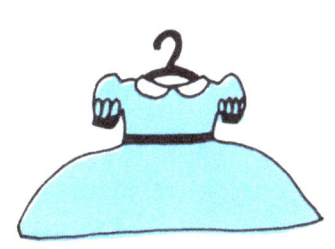

6

7

8

85

☐ a flock of trucks
☐ a flock of ducks

☐ a stack of blocks
☐ a stack of bricks

☐ many black tacks
☐ many black tracks

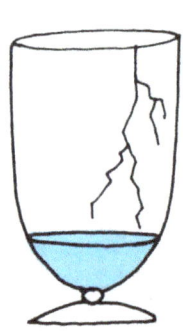

☐ a stick in the grass
☐ a crack in the glass

☐ The clock is black.
☐ The truck is stuck.

☐ A class can spell.
☐ A glass can spill.

☐ Press it.
☐ Dress it.

☐ Drill it.
☐ Spill it.

☐ Clock it.
☐ Crack it.

☐ Spell it.
☐ Smell it.

☐ Stuff it.
☐ Stack it.

☐ Stuff it.
☐ Sniff it.

☐ The doll has a silk dress.

☐ The doll has a big drill.

☐ The dolls can have a snack.

☐ The dogs can get the sticks.

☐ The duck's bill can go snip-snap.

☐ The drum's sticks can go click-clack.

☐ The trunk has blocks and a truck in it.

☐ The trunk has stems and sticks in it.

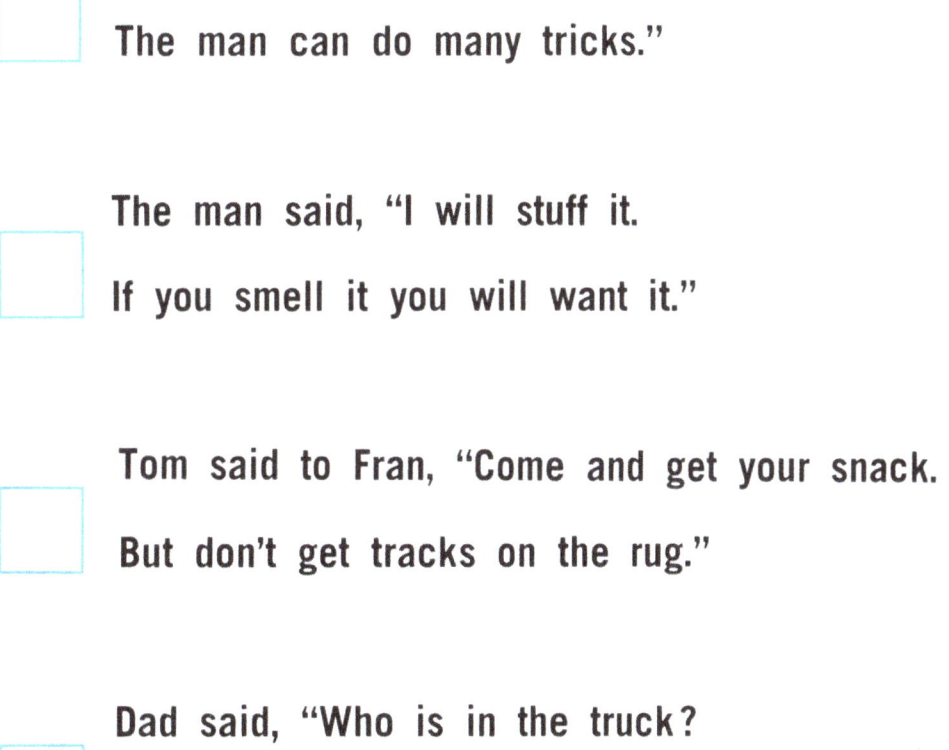

☐ Glen said, "The glass of milk won't spill.
The man can do many tricks."

☐ The man said, "I will stuff it.
If you smell it you will want it."

☐ Tom said to Fran, "Come and get your snack.
But don't get tracks on the rug."

☐ Dad said, "Who is in the truck?
It's stuck in the grass."

Fred said, "Let's go into the Big Top. We don't want to miss any swell

bricks."   tracks."   tricks."

"Here is my truck," said Dick. It can help us pick up the

flocks."   blocks."   locks."

Fran said, "Here comes the milkman! The milk is in his

track."   trick."   truck."

Mother said to Fran, "I am glad you are back from your class. "Don't trip on that

stack."   smack."   stick."

☐ Fred stuck a stick into the mud.

☐ Fred has a stack of sticks in his hand.

☐ A stack of blocks is in the box.

☐ A flock of black ducks is in the pond.

☐ The sticks will go click-clack and rat-a-tat.

☐ The clock will go tick-tock.

☐ Fred held the glass so that it could not spill.

☐ Fred held up his hand in class so that he could spell.

Yes and No

APTZE

They help you to spell,
  but do they help you to smell?

Yes____   No____

It runs on a track,
  but can it run on a crack?

Yes____   No____

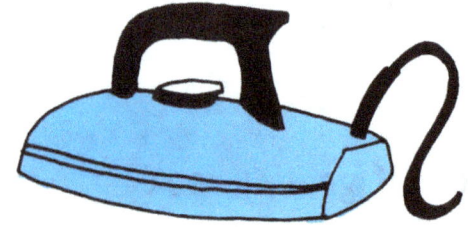

It will press your dress,
  but will it press a mess?

Yes____   No____

It can trim the grass,
  but can it cut a glass?

Yes____   No____

Is it in the class?

Fred Stan Fran Bess

	Yes	No
1. a dress on a doll	☐	☐
2. a twig in the grass	☐	☐
3. a snack on her desk	☐	☐
4. a list in Fred's hand	☐	☐
5. six sums to do	☐	☐
6. a big clock	☐	☐
7. blocks in a stack	☐	☐

It must be cut.

It is damp at sunup.

It is fun to rest on it.

Is it
- a dress
- a class
- grass

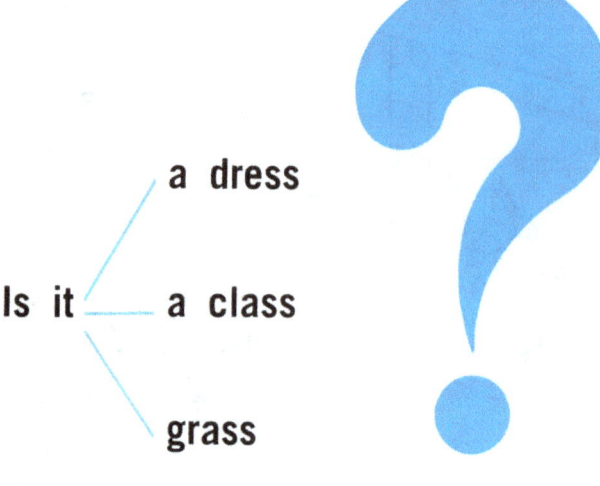

Its hands are not still.

It has some glass on it.

It should not stop.

Is it
- a flock
- a clock
- a block

9

It can have milk in it.

It can crack.

Mom said, "You should have held it in two hands."

Is it
- grass
- a class
- a glass

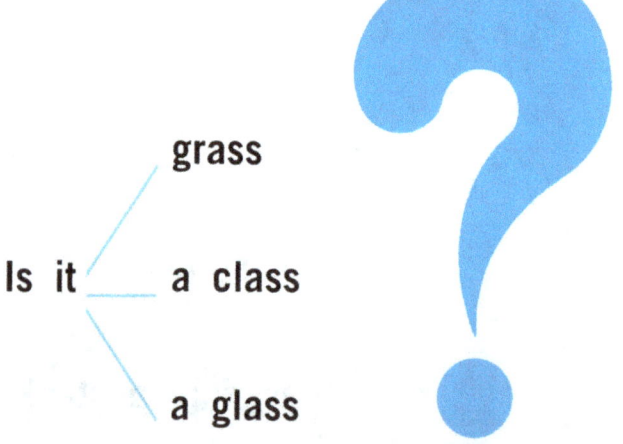

www.ingramcontent.com/pod-product-compliance
Lightning Source LLC
Chambersburg PA
CBHW081501070526
44586CB00019B/2445